Spanish Armada Tracts. No. 1

A Letter

Written on October 4, 1589

By

Captain Cuellar

of the Spanish Armada

To

His Majesty King Philip II

Recounting His Misadventures in Ireland and Elsewhere
after the Wreck of His Ship

TRANSLATED FROM THE ORIGINAL SPANISH BY

HENRY DWIGHT SEDGWICK, JR.

New York

George H. Richmond & Co.

1895

Copyright, 1895, by
GEORGE H. RICHMOND & CO.

Note

ON the 28th and 29th days of May, 1588, the Invincible Armada set sail from the mouth of the Tagus under the command of the Duke of Medina Sidonia, to conquer England, dethrone Elizabeth, and restore the Apostolic Roman Catholic faith. It met contrary winds, and was driven back to Spain. A second time it put forth, and on July 22d sailed from Corunna. In eight *days a favourable wind brought the* SAN MARTIN, *the flagship, which had lagged behind to guard the slowest vessels, in sight of the English coast. On July 31st, Howard and Drake attacked the Spanish fleet; from that day on there was a constant running fight up the Channel to Calais, where the Spaniards anchored on August 6th. The Armada's plan was to protect the Prince of Parma and his army during the passage of their transport boats from Dunkirk to England. On the 8th, the English fleet forced the fighting and won a complete victory. On* the 9th, the broken *Armada* was flying from the English up the North Sea, hoping to escape by doubling the north ends of Scotland and Ireland, and out into the *Atlantic*, and so homeward to Spain. Mr. Froude has given a brilliant description of these events in " The Spanish Story of the *Armada*." His essay does not pretend to be the result of any original investigation; it is wholly taken from a book entitled " La *Armada* Invencible," published in Madrid in 1885 by El Capitan Cesáreo Fernandez Duro. This book is mainly a compilation of *various documents, such as letters from the Duke of Medina Sidonia to Philip II., preserved in the Spanish archives and not before published. Among these documents is the following letter from Captain Cuellar, one of the officers in the Armada, to Philip II. In his narrative Froude gives an abridgment of it, but the letter seems worthy to be read at length.*

A Letter written by Captain Cuellar To His Majesty King Philip II.

Letter written on October 4, 1589, by Captain Cuellar of the Spanish Armada to His Majesty King Philip II, recounting his misadventures in Ireland and elsewhere after the wreck of his ship.

I BELIEVE that your Majesty will be surprised at seeing this letter on account of the little certainty which you could have had that I was alive, and I write that your Majesty may be sure of that, and somewhat at length. There is excuse enough that this letter

should be long, because of
the very great hardships and
misfortunes that I have under-
gone since the Armada sailed
from Lisbon for England,
from which God in His Infi-
nite Mercy has delivered me.
As I have found no opportunity for more than a year to
write to your Majesty, I have
not done so until now that God
has brought me to this land of
Flanders, whither I came may
be twelve days ago in company with the Spaniards
who escaped from the ships
that were wrecked off Ireland, Scotland, and Shetland.
There were more than twen-

ty of them, the largest in
the fleet, and on board was
much of the choicest infantry,
captains, ancients, colonels,
and other officers, also many
gentlemen and persons of
quality; and out of them all
— and there were more than
two hundred — not five escaped all told. Some were
drowned and the rest who
were able to swim ashore
were killed by the English
garrisons which the Queen
keeps in Ireland. By com-
mitting myself verily to God
and to the Holy Virgin, I escaped from the sea and from
these enemies, together with

three hundred odd soldiers who also were able to save themselves and swim ashore. With them I went through great misfortunes. Barefoot and naked all the winter, I spent more than seven months in mountains and woods and amongst savages, for in that part of Ireland where we were wrecked they are all such.

It does not seem to me right to refrain from telling your Majesty, nor to keep back the injustice and grievous injuries which some sought to do me so wrongfully, and without any fail-

ure on my part to do what
it was my duty to do.
From this God delivered me,
though I was condemned to
a shameful death, as your
Majesty knows. For, observ-
ing the severity with which
orders were given to carry
out the sentence, I demand-
ed with much boldness and
indignation to know the
cause why such injury and
insults were done to me,
seeing that I had served the
King as a good soldier and
loyal subject on every occasion and in every fight which
we had with the enemy's
fleet, from which my galleon

always came off having fared
very ill with many men killed
and wounded. I asked that
a copy of the orders should
be given to me, and that inquiry be made of the three
hundred and fifty men who
were on the galleon, and that
if any one should lay blame
on me, they should cut me
in four quarters. They would
not listen to me, nor to many
gentlemen who interceded for
me, answering that the Duke
at that time kept his cabin
and was very unhappy and
did not want anybody to
speak to him. For besides
the ill-success he always had

with the enemy, on the day of my tribulation he had been told that the two galleons, *San Mateo* and *San Felipe*, those from Portugal, on board which were two colonels, Don Francisco de Toledo, brother to the Count of Orgaz, and Don Diego Pimental, brother to the Marquis of Tavara, had been destroyed and sunk, and almost all hands drowned. For this reason the Duke kept himself in his cabin, and his Councilors did acts of injustice right and left in order to correct his neglect, disregarding the lives and honours of those that were not to blame, and that is so public that everybody knows it.

The galleon *San Pedro*, aboard which I was, sustained much hurt from some big cannon balls that the enemy shot into her on every side, and though repairs were made immediately as well as could be done, some hole still remained undiscovered and much water leaked in. And after the hard fight that we had off Calais on the eighth of August, which was the last of all, and continued from morning till seven o'clock at night, our fleet was drawing off—I don't know how to put it—and the enemy's fleet was following at our stern to drive us away from the English coast, and after we had retreated and were out of danger—it was now the tenth of August—and saw that the enemy held off, some of our ships began making repairs and patching their injuries ; and on that day, for my sins, I was taking a little rest, for I had not slept or taken time to attend to the necessities of life for ten days, when my scoundrel of a mate, without saying anything to me, hoisted sail

and put out in front of the
Admiral's ship a matter of
two miles, in order to go on
with our repairs, just as other
ships had done, and just
when he was lowering the
sails to see where the galleon
leaked, a tender came along-
side, and word was given me
from the Duke that I should
go to the Admiral's ship.
Thither I went, but before I
got there, an order was given
that I and another gentleman, Don Christobal de Avila,
who was captain of a victu-
aler that had gone much further ahead than my galleon,
should be put to death in dis-

grace. When I heard this severe sentence I thought to
burst into a passion, asking
all to bear witness to the
gross injustice that was done
me, since I had served so
well, as could be seen by
written proofs. Of all this,
the Duke heard nothing, for
he was, as I say, shut up
in his cabin. My lord Don
Francisco de Bovadilla was
the only one who gave or-
ders on board the fleet, and
everything was directed by
him and some others, and
their doings are well known.
He commanded me to be
brought to the Judge Advo-

cate's ship in order that whatever he saw fit should be inflicted upon me. Thither I went, and although the Judge Advocate, Martin de Aranda, for that was his name, was severe, he listened to me and made inquiry about me in secret and found that I had served your Majesty like a good soldier, and therefore he did not dare to execute upon me the order that he had received. He wrote to the Duke about it, and said that unless he received orders from him in writing signed by his own hand he would not execute the sentence, be-

cause he saw that there was
no cause for it, and that I was
guilty of nothing. And together with his, I wrote a letter to the Duke which made
him think well of the matter, and he sent answer to
the Judge Advocate that he
should not execute the sentence upon me, but upon
Don Christobal, whom they
hanged with great cruelty and
insult, considering that he
was a gentleman and known
to many. God was pleased
to deliver me on account of
my innocence, which your
Majesty can readily learn or
will have learned from many

persons who were witnesses of it. ° The Judge Advocate always showed me much kindness. I stayed aboard his ship, in which we underwent all the terrors of death; for from the storm that sprang up it leaked so much that it was full of water all the time, and we could not keep it pumped dry. We had no succour, nor any help except in God; for the Duke still stayed below, and the whole fleet went scattered before the storm in such manner that some ships went to Germany, others put to the islands of Holland and Zealand, falling into the hands of our enemy, some went to Shetland, others to Scotland, where they were wrecked and burned. More than twenty were lost off Ireland, with all the flower and chivalry of the fleet. As I have said, the ship on which I went belonged to the Levantine Squadron, and two other large ships kept us company, in order to help us if they could. On board one of them was Don Diego Enriquez, the hunchback, a colonel. He was unable to double Cape Clear in Ireland, on account of the bad storm that rose in front, and was

obliged to put for land with
those three ships, which, as I
say, were very big, and to
cast anchor more than half a
league from land, where we
remained for four days without
making any repairs, nor could
we do so ; and on the fifth,
up came a great storm upon
our beam, in terrible hurly-
burly, so that our cables could
not hold, nor were the sails of
any use; and with all three
ships we were driven on a
sandy beach surrounded on
every side by great rocks, a
most terrible spectacle; and in
the space of one hour all the
ships were dashed to pieces,

and not three hundred men escaped. More than a thousand were drowned, and among them many persons of rank, captains, gentlemen, and others. Don Diego died there more pitifully than ever was seen in this world; for, in fear of the boisterous waves that swept over the ship, he took his tender, which had a deck, and he together with the Count of Villafranca's son and two others, Portuguese gentlemen, taking more than sixteen thousand ducats' worth of jewels and crowns, got down below the deck of the tender, and had the hatchway fastened down over them and calked. Then immediately over seventy men who were still alive threw themselves from the ship on to the tender, and while that was struggling to make its way to shore, a great wave came over it, which sunk it and washed off all hands that were on it. And straightway the tender went tossing with the waves hither and thither, until it reached the beach, where it stuck fast upside down, and by this mishap the gentlemen who got under the little deck perished within. After the tender had been aground a

day and a half, some savages
came to it and rolled it over
in order to take out some nails
and bits of iron, and breaking
the deck they took out the
dead men. Don Diego Enriquez breathed his last in their
hands. They stripped him
and took the jewels and
money that there were, let-
ting the bodies lie there without burial. And because it is
a matter for wonderment and
true beyond doubt, I have
wished to tell it to your Majesty, and also that people in
Spain might know in what
manner that gentleman died;
and, moreover, as it would

not be just not to tell my
good hap and how I got
ashore, I go on.

I commended myself to
God and to our Lady, and
went aft to the top of the
ship's poop, and from thence
I looked about on the great
spectacle of woe. Many
men were sinking in the
ships ; others, throwing themselves into the water, went
down and never came up ;
some were on rafts and water-
casks ; captains threw their
gold chains and their money
into the sea, and some gentlemen I saw clinging to spars ;
others left on the ships cried

aloud, calling upon God; and some were swept off by waves which took them right out of the ships. And as I was staring at this horror, I knew not what to do or what part to take, for I cannot swim, and the waves and the storm were very great; and on the other hand, the land and the beach were full of enemies who were going about skipping and dancing for joy at our misfortune. Whenever any of our men reached land, two hundred savages and other enemies rushed upon them and stripped them of everything they wore, leaving them stark naked, and without any pity beat them and ill used them. All this could be plainly seen from the wrecked ships, and not a single good thing on any side did I see. I went up to the Judge Advocate—may God have mercy on him—he was very sad and downcast, and I bade him try to do something that might help save his life before the ship should break up completely, as it could not last more than ten minutes; and in fact it did not. Most of the people aboard and all the captains and officers had been

drowned before I cast about
for a means to save my life.
I got on a plank which had
broken off the ship, and the
Judge Advocate followed me,
laden with crowns which he
carried sewed into his doublet and hose ; but there was
no way to loose this plank
from the side of the ship, for
it was fastened by some big
iron chains, and the waves
and floating spars beat against
it, and inflicted upon us the
pangs of death. I tried another means of rescue, and
that was to catch hold of a
scuttle-board as large as a
good-sized table, which the

mercy of God happened to
bring to my hand ; but when
I tried to get on it I sank six
fathoms under water, and
swallowed so much that I
was almost drowned. When
I came up I called to the
Judge Advocate and managed
to pull him on the scuttle-
board with me; but as we
were getting clear of the ship,
a monstrous wave came up
and swept over us so hard
that the Judge Advocate could
not hold on, and the wave
carried him with it, and he
was drowned. As he went
down he shrieked aloud, calling upon God. I could not

help him, because when the board was left with the weight on only one side, it began to twirl around with me, and at that moment a log of wood almost broke my legs, but I mustered up courage, and climbed well up on the scuttle, praying to our Lady of Ontañar. Four waves came, one after the other, and without my knowing how nor being able to swim, they carried me ashore, where I landed; but I could not stand up, for I was all bruised and bleeding. The enemy and savages who were on the beach stripping all those who

had succeeded in swimming
ashore, seeing my plight,
legs, hands, and linen hose
all bloody, did not touch me
nor did they come up to me,
and so I crawled along, little by
little, as best I could. I passed
many Spaniards completely
naked without any clothes
on at all, shivering with the
cold, which was very severe.
The night came upon me in
this dreary place, and I was
obliged to lie down upon
some rushes in the field in
spite of the pain I suffered;
and then a gentleman came
up to me, naked, a very gen-
tle youth. He was so fright-

ened that he could not speak, not even to tell me who he was. At that hour, which was about nine o'clock at night, the wind died down and the sea was becoming calm. I was wet to the skin and half dead with pain and hunger, when two men came by, one with some weapon and the other with a great iron axe in his hands, and walked up to me and my companion. We lay still, as if nothing had been the matter with us, and they had compassion on seeing us, and without saying a word cut down some rushes and grasses and covered us up very well. Then they went to the beach to break open and loot the chests and whatever else they found, and in this they were assisted by over two thousand savages and Englishmen who were stationed in the garrisons round about. By managing to lie quiet a little, I fell asleep, until in the best of my slumber, about one o'clock in the morning, I was woke by a great noise of people on horseback, more than two hundred, who were on their way to pillage the ships. I turned to call my comrade to see if he

slept, and found that he was
dead, at which I was very
sad. I learned afterward
that he was a gentleman of
quality. There he lay on the
field with more than six hundred other bodies which the
sea had cast up. The crows
and the wolves fed upon
them, and there was nobody
to bury any of them, not even
poor Don Diego Enriquez.
At daybreak I began to go
a little at a time in quest
of a monastery of monks, in
order to get well there as
best I might. I reached the
place with much pain and suf-
fering, and found the monas-

tery torn down, the church
and holy images burned,
and everything destroyed,
and twelve Spaniards hanged
within the church by the
English Protestants, who
went about looking for us in
order to kill all those who
had escaped the hazard of the
sea. All the monks had fled
to the mountains for fear of
the enemy; for they would
have killed them too if they
had caught them, as is their
usage, not leaving a church
nor a hermitage standing, for
they have pulled them all
down and turned them into
drinking-sties for cows and

pigs. I write this in such detail that your Majesty may learn the adventures and hardships that I have seen, for your Majesty may occupy yourself a little by way of amusement after dinner in reading this letter, for it might almost seem to be taken out of some book of Knight Errantry. As I found nobody in that monastery except the Spaniards dangling from the iron grates in the church windows, I went out very quick and took a path that led through a wood. After I had gone along it about a mile, I met a woman, a wild savage, more than eighty years old, who was driving five or six cows to hide them in the wood, so that the English who had come to lodge in her village should not take them. When she saw me she stopped, and recognizing me said, "You Spain?" I told her by signs that I was, and that I had been wrecked on the ships. She had much pity upon me and began to cry, making signs to me that we were near her cabin and that I should not go thither, because many of the enemy were there, and they had cut off the heads of many Spaniards. All this was trial and tribulation for me, because I was all alone and badly lamed by a log that had almost broken my legs in the water. Finally, by the old woman's advice, I made up my mind to go back to the beach where the ships had been wrecked three days before. There were troops of people going about there, loading the spoils upon carts and carrying them to their huts. I did not dare show myself nor go up to them, lest they should strip off the wretched linen garments I had on my back, or murder

me; and then I saw two
poor Spanish soldiers come
along, naked as on the day
they were born, moaning and
calling to God to help them.
One had a bad cut on his
head, which he got when
they stripped him. I called
to them from where I was
hid, and they came up to me
and told me of the cruel
deaths and tortures that the
English had inflicted upon
more than a hundred Span-
iards whom they had cap-
tured. I had sorrow enough
for this news, but God gave
me strength, and after I had
commended myself to Him

and to His blessed Mother, I said to the two soldiers, "Let us go to the ships where those people are plundering; perhaps we shall find something to eat and drink, for I am surely starving to death." And going thither we saw dead bodies—and great pain and pity it was to see them— for the sea was still throwing them up, and more than four hundred lay stiff upon the sand. We recognized some of them, among others poor Don Diego Enriquez; and in spite of my forlorn condition, I could not bear to pass him by without burying him, and so we dug a hole in the sand by the water's edge. There we laid him with another much honoured captain, a dear friend of mine; and we had hardly finished covering them with earth when some two hundred savages came up to see what we were doing. We told them by signs that we had buried these men there so that the crows should not eat them, as they were our brothers. Then we set out to look for something to eat along the beach, for the sea had cast up some biscuits, when four savages rushed up to me to tear the

clothes off my back; but another man, when he saw
them begin to maltreat me,
took pity on me, and sent
them off. He must have
been a man of rank, because
they obeyed him. Then, by
the grace of God, he lent as-
sistance to me and my two
companions, and took us
away from there, and tarried
a long time with us until he
put us on a road that went
away from the shore and led
to a village where he lived.
He told us to wait for him
there, for he would soon
come back and show us our
path for some way on. This

road was very stony, and I could not stir nor take a step forward because I was bare-foot and half dead with pain in my leg which had a very deep cut. My poor compan-ions were naked and stiff with cold, which was very bitter; and as they could not bear it nor be of any help to me, they went ahead along the road, and I remained there praying to God for help. He came to my aid, and I began to walk, little by little, and reached a high place from whence I could see some straw huts. I went toward these through a dell, and entered a wood; and after I had gone the distance of two musket-shots through it, a man over seventy years old came out from behind some rocks, and with him two young men carrying arms, one an Englishman and the other a Frenchman, and also a very pretty girl of twenty, all of whom were going to the shore to plunder. When they saw me walking through the trees they came toward me, and the Englishman, running up, cried, "Surrender, you Spanish coward!" and made a cut at me with his knife, trying to kill me. I parried the blow with a stick I had in my hand, but he succeeded in hitting me and cut me in the right leg. He would have struck me again if the old savage and his daughter, who was probably the Englishman's mistress, had not come up. I bade him do what he would with me, since fortune had vanquished me and taken away my arms in the sea. They separated him from me, and the savage stripped me even to my shirt. Under it I wore a gold chain worth more than a thousand reals. When they saw this they

were delighted and rummaged
through my doublet thread
by thread. In this I carried
forty-five gold crowns which
had been given me at Co-
runna by the Duke's orders
for two months' pay. When
the Englishman saw that I
had a gold chain and money,
he wanted to keep me prisoner, thinking that he would
be offered a ransom for me.
I told him that I had nothing
to give, as I was only a poor
soldier, and that I had got
that gold aboard ship. The
girl was very sorry to see the
ill usage they did me, and en-
treated them to give me back

my clothes and do me no
more harm. They all went
back to the savage's cabin,
and I was left under the trees,
bleeding fast from the cut that
the Englishman had given me.
I put on my doublet and coat.
They had even taken away
my shirt and some precious
relics which I wore in a little
jacket of the brotherhood of
the Holy Trinity, and which
had been given to me at Lisbon. The girl took these and
put them around her neck,
making signs to me that she
wished to keep them, and telling me that she was a Christian, and so she was—like

Mahomet. They sent a boy to me from the hut bearing a poultice made of herbs to put on my wound, also milk, butter, and a piece of oaten bread for me to eat. I poulticed myself and ate. Then the boy went with me along the road, pointing out the direction in which I ought to go, and keeping me away from a village which was in sight of the road, where many Spaniards had been killed, and not a single man on whom the inhabitants could lay hands had escaped. The Frenchman was the cause of doing me this good turn, for he had

been a soldier at Terceira, and
he was very sorry to see me
so maltreated. When the
boy turned to go back, he
bade me keep straight on to
some mountains that seemed
to be some six leagues from
us, behind which lay a friendly country that belonged to a
great lord who was a good
friend to the King of Spain,
and who harboured all the
Spaniards that came to him,
and was very kind to them,
and had taken in more than
eighty of the men from our
ships who had gone to him
naked. At this news I
plucked up courage some-

what, and stick in hand started to walk as best I could, striking north for the mountains that the boy had pointed out. That night I came to some huts where they did me no harm because there was a young man there who knew Latin, and God was pleased that owing to the necessity of the occasion we should understand one another in that language. I told him my misfortunes. The Latin scholar took me into his hut for the night, and gave me medicine and some supper and a place on the straw to sleep. In the

middle of the night his father
and brothers came home
laden with the spoils of our
things, but the old man did
not mind that they had taken
me into his house and had
treated me well. In the
morning they gave me a boy
and a horse to take me over
a mile of road which was so
bad that the mud was up to
the horse's pasterns. After
we had gone past it by a bow-
shot we heard a great noise,
and the boy said to me, making signs, "Save yourself,
Spain," for that is what they
call us. "Many Saxons are
coming on horseback, and

they will kill you unless you hide. Come here quick!" They call the English Saxons. We hid in the cleft of some rocks, where we lay safe without being seen. There were more than one hundred and fifty of them on horseback, and they were going all along the coast to rob and kill all the Spaniards that they could find. God delivered me from them, but as we went on our way we met more than forty savages on foot who wanted to murder me, for they were all Protestants, but they did not do it because the boy who was with me told them that his master had captured me and I was his prisoner, and that he was sending me on horseback so that I might get well. All this did not suffice to secure my going on in peace, for two of those robbers seized me and gave me half a dozen blows, bruising my back and arms, and stripped me of everything I had on, and left me naked as when I was born. By the Holy Baptism that I received, this is true. Then, seeing myself in this plight, I gave thanks to God, supplicating His Divine Majesty to fulfil His will upon me, for that was my will also. The savage's boy then turned to go home with his horse, weeping to see me so naked, beaten, and cold. I besought God very earnestly to take me where I might confess myself and then die in His grace. Then I plucked up courage, being in the worst extreme of misfortune that ever a man was, and covered myself with some fern leaves and a bit of an old mat, and protected myself from the cold the best I could. I journeyed on, little by little, in a direction they had pointed out, in search of the lands of that chieftain with whom the other Spaniards had taken refuge, and I came to that peak which they had pointed out as a mark. There I found a lake around which there were some thirty huts, all completely empty, and I looked about for a place to spend the night. Having nowhere to go, I went up to the biggest cabin, as that seemed the best place to take shelter in for the night, for all of them were deserted and empty. As I was going in the door I saw there many bundles of oats, which are made into the bread that

those savages usually eat, and
I thanked God that on them
I had a good place to sleep,
when of a sudden I saw three
naked men get up at one side,
and come forward and stare
at me. It gave me a start, for
I thought without doubt they
were devils, and they knew
no better what I could be,
wrapped up in my mat and
leaves. They were so fright-
ened that they did not speak
to me, nor I to them, and I
could not see them distinctly,
for the hut was rather dark;
and being much confounded
I exclaimed, "Oh, Mother of
God, be with me and deliver

me from all evil." When
they heard me speak Span-
ish and call on the Mother
of God, they also exclaimed,
"Holy Virgin, be with us."
Then I was reassured, and
went up to them and ask-
ed if they were Spaniards.
They answered, "Yes, we
are, for our sins. Eleven of
us together were robbed of
everything on the beach, and
naked as we were we went
to look for some place where
Christians dwelt, and on the
way we met a troop of the
enemy, who killed eight of
us. The three of us here escaped into a wood which was

so thick that they could not
find us, and that night God
led us thither to these huts,
and here we stayed to re-
cover from our fatigue, although there were no people
and nothing to eat." I told
them always to commit
themselves to God and to be
of good cheer, for we were in
the neighbourhood of friends
and Christians, for I had information of a village that
was about three or four
leagues away from us, which
belonged to my Lord Ruerque
(O'Rourke), where many of
the wrecked Spaniards had
taken refuge, and that al-

though I was very badly used
up and wounded we should
start on our journey thither
the next day. The poor fellows were delighted, and
asked me who I was. I told
them that I was Captain Cuellar. They could hardly believe it, for they thought I
was drowned, and rushed up
to me and hugged me almost
to death. One of them was
a sergeant and the other two
common soldiers. And as
this tale is ludicrous, and
true as I am a Christian, I
have written it all out for
your Majesty's diversion. I
buried myself deep in the

straw, taking care not to disturb it or disarrange it from
the way it was ; and, having
agreed to get up early in
the morning for our journey,
we went to sleep without
supper, and without having
had anything to eat except
mulberries and water-cress.
While it was still daytime I
was already wide awake with
a great pain in my legs, and I
heard noises and talking, and
just then a savage came to
the door with a battle-axe in
his hand, and looked around
at the oats, muttering to himself. I and my companions,
who had also waked up,

lay still without drawing
a breath, peering attentively
through the straw at the savage to see what he would do.
God willed that he went out
and betook himself, with a
number of others who had
come with him, to work at
reaping near the huts, in such
a place that it was impossible
for us to go out without their
seeing us. We lay still, buried alive, talking over what
we had better do, and agreed
not to get out of the straw
or to move from that place as
long as those savages and
heretics were there; for they
belonged to that neighbour-

hood where the people treated the poor Spaniards whom
they caught so dreadfully,
and they would have done
the like to us if they had
found us there, where there
was no one to help us but
God. All day passed in this
way, and when night came
those wretches betook themselves to their huts. We
waited for the moon to rise,
and then, wrapped up in straw
and hay, because it was bitter cold, we left that dan-
gerous place without waiting
for daylight. We went on,
floundering in the mud, half
dead with pain, hunger, and

thirst. God was pleased to bring us to a land of some safety where we found a hamlet belonging to better people, although they were all savages, yet Christians and kindly. One of them saw my wound and in what bad plight I was, and took me into his hut, and he and his wife and children took care of me, and he would not let me go till he thought that I could safely reach the village whither I was going. In that village I found more than seventy Spaniards. They had no clothes and were very ill treated, because the chief was

not there : he had gone to
defend a part of the country which the English were
coming to attack ; for although he is a savage he is a
very good Christian and an
enemy to the heretics, and
always fights against them.
His name is Lord de Ruerge
(O'Rourke).   I reached his
house with much difficulty,
covered with straw and a bit
of mat twined around my
body, so that everybody was
moved with pity at seeing me.
Some of the savages gave
me a wretched old cloak full
of lice, which I put on and
found of some comfort.   Next

day, in the morning, some
twenty of us Spanish met together at Chief Ruerque's hut,
asking them to give us something to eat for love of God,
and as we stood begging they
informed us that there was a
very large Spanish ship on
the coast, which had come
for the Spaniards who had
escaped. At this news, without waiting, all twenty of us
set out for the place where
we were told the ship was.
We found many obstacles on
the way, but that was a good
thing for me, and a mercy
that God did to me, in that
I did not reach the harbour

where the ship was, as the others that were with me did. The ship belonged to the fleet, and had put into port there in a great storm with the mainmast and rigging in a very bad condition. They were afraid lest the enemy, who were getting ready with great vigour, should burn the ship or do it some other harm, so they made repairs in two days' time, and then, with the people that came in her and those besides whom they picked up, they sailed off and again ran aground on the same coast, and more than two hundred persons were drowned. Those who escaped by swimming ashore were captured by the English and put to the sword. God was pleased that I alone should be left out of the twenty who went to look for the ship, so that I should not suffer like the others. Blessed be His holy mercy forever for all the mercies He has shown me. Having thus lost my way, I was going in great perplexity and trouble when I struck a road and met a clerk in a lay habit walking along, for the priests in that country travel in that way so that the English shall not recognize them.

He took pity on me, and spoke to me in Latin, and asked me of what nation I was and about the shipwrecks through which I had passed. God gave me grace so that I could answer about everything which he asked me in the same Latin tongue. He was so satisfied with me that he gave me to eat from what he carried with him, and set me on a road by which I should get to a castle that was about six leagues from there. He said it was a very strong place, and belonged to a savage chief, a very valiant soldier and a great enemy of the Queen of England and of everything that was hers, a man who would never obey or pay tribute, keeping himself in his castle and among the mountains that made his stronghold. Thither I went, overcoming many difficulties by the way: that which was the worst and did me most harm was that a savage met me on the road and by a cheat took me to his hut in a desert valley, and told me that I had to live with him all my life, and that he would teach me his trade, which was a blacksmith's. I did not know what to answer him, nor did I dare lest he should put me in the forge. On the contrary, I assumed a cheerful face and went to work at the bellows for more than eight days. The wicked blacksmith was pleased with this, for I worked carefully so as not to vex him, and so was the accursed old woman his wife. I was getting very sad and downhearted over this occupation when God came to my help by sending the priest back that way. He was shocked to see me, but the savage would not let me go as he wanted my services. The priest rebuked him roundly, and bade me not to be troubled for he should speak to the Lord of the Castle whither he had directed me, and should get him to send for me. And so he did the next day, because this chief sent four of his adherents, savages, and a Spanish soldier, for he had with him ten of those who had swum ashore from the wreck. When he saw me without any clothes and dressed in straw, he and all who were with him felt very sorry, and the women wept to see me so ill used. They made me amends as well as they could with a woolen blanket after their fashion, and there I stayed three months, turned into a savage just like them. My master's wife was exceedingly comely and was very good to me, and one day we sat together in the sun, she and friends of hers and relations. They questioned me about Spain and other places, and finally asked me to look at their hands and tell them their fortunes. I rendered thanks to God, for now that I was become a gipsy among savages, there was nothing further to befall me. I examined all their hands, and told them a hundred thousand nonsensical things, at which they were mightily pleased, so that no other Spaniard stood so high in their regard as I, and both day and night men and women followed me about incessantly to have me tell their fortunes, so that I was surrounded by such a crowd that I was compelled to ask permission of my master to leave his castle. He would not grant it, but gave orders that. no one should disturb me or give me any annoyance.

The nature of these savages is to live like beasts among the mountains, some of which are very rugged in the parts of the island where we were cast away. They live in huts made of straw. The men have big bodies, their features and limbs are well made, and they are agile as deer. They eat but one meal a day, and that at night, and their ordinary food is oaten bread and butter. They drink sour milk, as they have no other beverage, but no water, although it is the best in the world. On holidays they eat meat, half cooked, without bread or salt.

They dress in tight breeches and goatskin jackets cut short but very big, and over all a blanket, and wear their hair down to their eyes. They are good walkers, and have great endurance. They are always at war with the English who garrison the country there, and both defend themselves from them and prevent them from coming into their territory, which is all flooded and covered with marshy ponds. Their domain spreads more than forty leagues each way. Their great bent is to be robbers and to steal from one

another, so that not a day
passes without a call to arms
among them. For when the
men of one hamlet learn that
there are cattle or anything
else in another, they go at
once, armed, by night, and
shouting war-whoops kill one
another, and then when the
English learn which village
has gathered in and stolen
most cattle they swoop down
on it and take all away;
and these have no other help
than to fly to the mountains
with their wives and flocks,
for they possess no other
property, neither household
stuff nor clothes. They sleep

on the ground, upon rushes
freshly cut and full of water
or else frozen stiff. Most of
the women are very pretty
but ill dressed. They wear
nothing but a shift and a
blanket over it, and a linen
cloth much folded on their
heads and tied in front. They
are hard workers and good
housewives after their fashion. These people call themselves Christians; they hear
mass and follow the usages
of the Catholic Church. Almost all their churches, mon-
asteries, and hermitages have
been destroyed by the soldiers from the English gar-

risons and by their own countrymen who have joined those, for they are as bad as the English. And to sum up, in that country there is neither justice nor right, and everybody does what he likes. These savages liked us very much, for they knew that we were great enemies to the heretics and had come against them, and had it not been for them not one of us would now be alive. We were very grateful to them for this, although they were the first to rob and plunder those of us who reached the land alive. These savages got a great quantity of jewels and money from us and from those thirteen ships of our fleet, for there were many people of great possessions on board them who were all drowned. News of this came to the Lord Governor of the kingdom, who was in the city of Dililin (Dublin), and he straightway set forth with seventeen hundred soldiers to look for the wrecks and for the people that had escaped, who were near a thousand, and were wandering about the country, without arms and without clothes, in the neighbourhood of the different places where the ships had been wrecked. The Governor captured most of them and hanged them at once, and did other acts of cruelty. He put in prison those who were said to have given us succour, and did them all the evil he could. He took prisoners three or four chieftains who possessed castles and had received some of the Spanish in them, and then marched all along the coast until he came to the place where I was wrecked, and from thence he made an incursion to Manglana's castle, for that was the name of the

savage with whom I lived.
This chieftain was always a
great enemy of the Queen's,
and never loved anything that
was hers, nor would he obey
her, and therefore the Governor wanted very much to
take him prisoner. When
this chief heard of the great
force that was coming against
him, knowing he had no
means of resistance, he resolved to fly to the mountains, which, in default of an
army, was his only safety.
We Spanish, who were with
him, already had news of the
evil that was coming upon
us, and we did not know

what to do nor where to turn for safety; and one Sunday, after mass, the chief blazing with anger, his hair hanging down over his eyes, took us apart, and said that he could not entertain any hope of defence, and that he had made up his mind to fly with all his people, their flocks and families, and that we must look to what we should do to save our lives. I made answer that if he would wait for a little we would quickly give him a reply. I withdrew apart with the eight Spaniards that were with me — they were brave fellows—and said to them that they could see clearly all the trials that we had passed, and that one which was coming upon us, and that in order not to undergo more it was better to die with honour once for all, and since we had a fair opportunity we should not wait longer, nor wander fugitives over the mountains, naked, barefoot, in the freezing cold, and since the savage had resolved to abandon his castle, we nine Spaniards who were there should merrily throw ourselves into it, and defend it to death. This we could well do against twice as

strong a force as that which
was coming, for the castle
was very stout, and very hard
to take unless they should
bombard it with artillery; for
it is built on a deep lake
more than a league wide in
some places, and three or
four leagues long, and has
an outlet to the sea, but
even when this is swollen by
spring tides there is no passage there. For this reason
the castle is safe from attack,
and is inaccessible both by
water and by the strip of land
that runs up to it, because
for a league around the village, which is built on solid

ground, lies a marsh deep as a man's chest, so that even the inhabitants cannot get to it except by certain paths. Having well considered all this, we made up our minds to tell the savage that we would man the castle and defend it to the death, and we asked him to furnish it as quickly as he could with provisions for six months and with arms. The chieftain was so pleased at this and at our courage that he lost no time in supplying the castle with the aid of the chief men of the village, at which all were much gratified. And in order to make sure that we should not play him false, he made us take an oath that we would not abandon his castle nor surrender it to the enemy upon any terms or conditions, although we should starve to death, and that we would not open the gates to let in any Irishman, or Spaniard, or anybody at all, until the chief should return in person, as he made no doubt that we would keep our promise. And after all the necessary things had been done, we put the ornaments and fineries from the church into the castle, and some relics that were there, and also laid in three or four boatloads of stones, half a dozen muskets, half a dozen arquebuses, and some other weapons. The chief embraced us and betook himself to the mountains, whither his people had already gone. And straightway word went all the country round how Manglana's castle was prepared for defence and would not surrender to the enemy, because it was garrisoned by a Spanish captain and some Spanish soldiers who were in it. Everybody admired our courage, and the enemy was very angry at what we had done, and marched against the castle with all their forces, some eighteen hundred men, and came within a mile and a half without being able to draw nearer by reason of the water that was all around it. From there they made great threats and hanged two Spaniards, and did other acts of violence in order to scare us. They summoned us many times by a trumpet to quit the castle, saying they would spare our lives and give us safe conduct to Spain. We bade them come nearer the tower, as we could not hear them plainly; and always showed that we recked little of their threats and promises. For seventeen days we were besieged. God was pleased to help us, and delivered us from our enemies by means of terrible storms and heavy snows that came upon them in such manner that they were forced to raise the siege and march back to Duplin (Dublin), where the Governor had his headquarters and garrison. From thence he sent us a threatening message that we had better look out for ourselves and not fall into his hands, and that he should come back to our region in good time. We sent him back an answer that made us laugh, and also our chieftain, who no sooner heard that the English had retreated than he returned to his castle and enjoyed quiet thereafter, giving us many presents. He proclaimed that we were most loyal friends, and offered to put all that was his at our service, and the chief men of the country did the like. He would have given me his own sister in marriage, but I thanked him very much, and contented myself with asking for guides to conduct me

somewhere where I could
find means of getting across
to Scotland. He would not
give me, nor any of the Spanish there, leave to go, saying
that the roads were not safe.
I did not relish such exces-
sive friendship, and so made
up my mind secretly, with
four of the soldiers that were
under my command, to set
out in the morning, two hours
before daybreak, so that no
one should stop our going. I
was the more determined because the day before one of
Manglana's sons had told me
that his father would not let
me leave the castle till the

King of Spain sent soldiers after me, and that he intended to imprison me so that I should not escape. At this news I accoutred myself as best I could, and started off with those four soldiers one morning ten days after Christmas in the year '88, and I went on journeying over mountains and through waste places, with great hardships, as God knows. After travelling twenty days, I reached the coast where Alonso de Leyva, Count de Paredes, and Don Tomas de Granvela had been wrecked, besides so many other gentlemen that a roll of paper would be needed to give a list of them. I went about among the huts of some savages that dwelt hard by, and they told me most pitiful tales of our people who had been drowned there, and they showed me many ornaments and rich garments that had belonged to them, at which I felt great grief, and all the more because I did not find any boat in which I could embark to go to Scotland. But one day they told me about a part of the country that belonged to a savage who called himself the Prince of Ocan, where there were

some vessels bound for Scotland. I journeyed there, crawl-
ing along the ground, for I
could not walk owing to the
wound on my leg; and as it
was a matter of life and death
to me, I put all there was in
me into going on ; but though
I got there as quick as I could,
the vessels had already sailed
two days before. This was
no small grief to me, for I was
in a wretched part of the
country surrounded by enemies, as there were many
English stationed at that harbour, and every day they paid
a visit to The Ocan. At this
time I was attacked with great

pain in my leg, so that I could not bear my weight on it at all, and the people warned me to be on the lookout, for there were many English there who would do me great harm, as they had done to other Spaniards, if they should catch me, and especially if they found out who I was. I did not know what to do, for the soldiers who came with me had already left me and had gone to another harbour further on to look for a ship, but some women, who saw that I was weak and forsaken, had compassion on me, and took me to their cabins in the mountains, and there they kept me for more than a month and a half, well guarded, and took such good care of me that my wound healed, and I felt in good condition to go to The Ocan's village to have an interview with him; but he would neither hear me nor see me, and I was told that he had pledged his word to the Queen's Lord Governor not to keep any Spaniards in his territory, nor to suffer any to go over it. After that the English who were stationed there marched off to make an attack upon some place, and The Ocan went with them, taking all his fighting men, so that I was free to wander about the village, which was made of thatched houses. There were some very pretty girls there with whom I was on friendly terms, and I used to go into their houses sometimes to gossip, until one evening two young Englishmen came in there. One of them was a sergeant and knew of me by name, but had never seen me. They sat down and asked me if I was not a Spaniard, and what I was doing there. I said yes, and that I was one of the soldiers in the com-

mand of Don Alonso de Lu-
çon, who had surrendered to
the English not long before,
and that by reason of a wound
in my leg I had not been able
to leave that place, and that
I was at their service and
ready to do whatever they
should be pleased to com-
mand. They bade me wait
for them a little while, for I
must go with them to the
city of Dublin, where there
were many Spanish gentle-
men of rank in prison. I said
that I could not walk, and
they sent in quest of a horse
to carry me, and I told them
that I was very content to do

their pleasure and to go with them. They entertained no suspicion of this, and began to flirt with the girls. Then the mother of these girls made signs to me to go out by the door, which I did with great agility, and made off, bounding down a ravine until I got into some thick briers, and I pushed through these till the castle of The Ocan was lost to sight. I went on in this way until nightfall, when I came to a large lake, and on the bank I saw a herd of cows. I went toward them to see if there were anybody there who could tell me where I was, and I met two young savages who were on their way to round up the cows and drive them high up on the mountains, where they and their fathers had taken refuge for fear of the English. I spent two days there with them, and they showed me great hospitality. It was necessary for one of the boys to go to the Prince of Ocan's village to learn the news, and there he saw those two Englishmen, who were going about in great rage looking for me, for some one had given them some information about me, and they asked every one who went by if they had seen me. The boy was such a good fellow that he returned to the hut and warned me of what was happening, and I felt it necessary for me to leave them very early in the morning to travel in search of a bishop who lived seven leagues from there in a castle, whither he had fled to seek refuge from the English. This bishop was a very good Christian. He used to go about dressed as a savage in order not to be discovered, and I assure your Majesty that I could not hold back my tears when I went up to him and kissed his hand. He had twelve Spaniards with him, meaning to help them to cross over to Scotland, and he was greatly pleased at my coming, especially when the soldiers told him that I was a captain. During the six days that I was with him he showed me all the hospitality he could, and had a small boat come with all preparations to take us over to Scotland, which trip was commonly made in two days. He gave us supplies for the sea, and said mass in the castle, and spoke with me about some matters concerning the loss of the kingdom, and how much your Majesty had helped them, and that I should try to go to Spain as fast as I could after landing in Scotland, where he advised me to live with great patience, because almost all the people there were Protestants, and very few Catholics. The bishop's name was Don Reimundo Termi [?], Bishop of Times [?], a noble and righteous man. May God keep him in his protection, and deliver him from his enemies. On the same day on the morning of which I reached the coast, I put to sea in a wretched pinnace in which there were eighteen of us, and that same day the wind was contrary, and we were obliged by God's mercy to run before it in the direction of Shetland [? Hebrides], where we reached land in the morning, our boat almost full of water and the mainsail torn. We went ashore and gave thanks to God for the mercies that he had shown us in bringing us there alive; and from there, after two days of good weather, we began our voyage to Scotland, which we reached in three days, not without danger because the leaky boat took in so much water. I praised God that He had plucked us out of so many great dangers and had brought me to a land where I might perhaps find better safety, for we were told that the King of Scotland would receive all the Spaniards that came to his kingdom, and would give them clothes and ships, so that they might go home to Spain. But everything was just the contrary, for he did not help any one, nor did he give away a crown in alms, in spite of the great need among those who had come to his kingdom. We had gone to Scotland to seek safety and a way of getting to Spain, and we stayed there for more than six months without any means, in just the condition that we had come in from Ireland and other places. I rather believe that the King had been persuaded on the part of the Queen of England to surrender us to her, and if the Catholic lords and noblemen of the country—for there are many of them and very noble gentlemen—had not espoused our cause and spoken in our behalf to the King

and in the councils that were
held on the matter, without
doubt we should have been
sold and delivered to the
English. For the King of
Scotland is nothing; he has
no authority, nor even the fig-
ure of a king, and does not
stir a step or eat a mouthful
but by the Queen's orders.
And thus there are great dis-
sensions among the nobility,
and some bear no good will
to him, but wish to see him
out of the way and your Majesty seated on his throne,
that you may establish the
Church of God, which is in
ruins there. This they said to

us many times with tears in their eyes, hoping that they will see it when it shall come to pass, and trusting to God that it may be soon. And as I say, these noblemen supported us all the time we were there, and gave us alms freely, and were very kind to us, entertaining great pity for our tribulations, and asked us to have patience and be long-suffering with the people that called us idolaters and bad Christians, and spoke a thousand insulting things to us; for if any one should make any answer, they would fall upon him and kill him. It was impossible to live or to stay in such a bad kingdom with such a bad king. [*The manuscript here is torn and illegible.*] . . . A special messenger was sent to the Duke of Parma . . . at which his Highness, like a pious prince, was much grieved, and with great diligence sought to help us . . . to the King that he should suffer us to depart freely from the country, and to the Catholics and friends great gratitude on the part of his Majesty, together with very friendly letters from him. There was a Scotch trader in Flanders who came forward

and agreed with his Highness
that he should come to Scotland for us and take us on
board four vessels, with all
necessary supplies, and con-
vey us to Flanders, and his
Highness was to pay five ducats for each Spaniard that he
carried to Flanders. The bar-
gain was made with him, and
he came for us and took us
aboard, without arms and
without clothes just as we
were, and carried us past the
English ports, which rendered
our passage safe from all the
English fleets and ships. But
this did us no good, for the
English had made terms with

the ships of Holland and Zealand that the latter should put to sea and lie in wait for us at the bar off Dunkirk, and there put us to the sword without leaving a single man alive. And this the Dutchmen did according to orders, for they were on the watch for us a month and a half in the port of Dunkirk, and there, if God had not helped us, they would have captured us all. But God willed that of the four vessels in which we came, two should escape. These ran ashore, where they split and were wholly wrecked, and the enemy, seeing the mode of escape we were after, opened a cannonade upon us, so that we were obliged to jump into the water and swim, and we thought to die there. They could not put out to our rescue from the port of Dunkirk in little boats, because the enemy kept up such a brisk fire. Moreover, the wind and waves were very high, so that we were in the greatest danger of perishing to a man. Nevertheless, we kept afloat on bits of wood, except some soldiers who were drowned, and also a Scotch captain. I got to land in my shirt, without any other clothes, and some soldiers from Medina [?] who were there came to my rescue. It was pitiful to see us enter the city a second time naked to the skin; and out to sea we saw under our very eyes the Dutch killing 270 Spaniards, who had come in the ship which they captured there off Dunkirk, not leaving but three alive. They are already paying the reckoning, however; for more than 400 Dutchmen have been captured since then and have had their heads chopped off. All this I have made bold to write to your Majesty.

From the City of Antwerp, the fourth of October, in the year 1589.

FRANCISCO DE CUELLAR.

[Academy of Hist. Investigation, Salazar, No. 7, page 58.]

CPSIA information can be obtained at www.ICGtesting.com
Printed in the USA
LVOW090227020512

279899LV00017BA/16/A